D-DAY

by

Wallace B. Black
and
Jean F. Blashfield

CRESTWOOD HOUSE
New York

Maxwell Macmillan Canada
Toronto

Maxwell Macmillan International
New York Oxford Singapore Sydney

Library of Congress Cataloging-in-Publication Data

Black, Wallace B.
    D-Day / by Wallace B. Black and Jean F. Blashfield. —
1st ed.
      p.   cm. — (World War II 50th anniversary series)
    Includes index.
    Summary: Describes the events leading up to the Allied invasion of Europe
— the last turning point in World War II.
    ISBN 0-89686-566-5
    1. World War, 1939-1945–Campaigns—France—Normandy—Juvenile
literature. 2. Normandy (France)—History—Juvenile literature. [1. World
War, 1939-1945—Campaigns—France—Normandy. 2. Normandy (France)—
History.] I. Blashfield, Jean F. II. Title. III. Series: Black, Wallace B.
World War II 50th anniversary.
D756.5.N6B5 1992
940.54'2142--dc20

          91-45951

Created and produced by B & B Publishing, Inc.

Picture Credits
Dave Conant, map - page 24
Imperial War Museum - page 26
National Archives - pages 8, 13, 17, 19, 23, 27, 28, 30, 31, 35, 36, 37, 39, 42, 43, 45
United States Air Force - pages 5, 12, 33, 40
United States Navy - pages 3, 7, 11, 15, 16, 20, 21

**CRESTWOOD
HOUSE**

Macmillan Publishing Company
866 Third Avenue
New York, NY 10022

Maxwell Macmillan Canada, Inc.
1200 Eglinton Avenue East
Suite 200
Don Mills, Ontario M3C 3N1

Macmillan Publishing Company is part of the Maxwell Communication Group of Companies.

Printed in the United States of America

First Edition

10 9 8 7 6 5 4 3 2 1

CONTENTS

Chapter 1

PLANNING FOR D-DAY

In September 1939 Germany attacked and conquered Poland. Coming to the aid of Poland, Great Britain and France declared war on Germany. World War II had begun.

After months of inactivity, Germany unleashed blitzkrieg (lightning war) attacks against the countries of western Europe. On June 5, 1940, at Dunkirk in France, British, French and Belgian armies were being driven into the sea. German panzers (tanks) and Luftwaffe (German air force) fighters and bombers by the thousands led the way for a conquering German army. Holland, Belgium, Luxembourg and France surrendered to the Germans.

In western Europe Great Britain was left alone to fight the Nazi armies. Fleets of Luftwaffe bombers rained bombs on England. An invasion by Adolf Hitler's victorious armies and the defeat of Great Britain seemed only days away.

Under the leadership of their courageous prime minister, Winston Churchill, the British began to fight back. The Battle of Britain, the great air battle between the Luftwaffe and the Royal Air Force (RAF), went on for months. London and other cities in Britain were bombed again and again. Hundreds of brave pilots of the RAF and thousands of British civilians lost their lives each month.

As winter of 1940 approached, the RAF Fighter Command won the Battle of Britain. Germany called off its plans for invasion. The RAF was gaining control of the skies over England. But even so, the Blitz — as the heavy bombing of British cities by the Luftwaffe was called — continued for another ten months.

An RAF Halifax heavy bomber over a German city. From 1941 to 1944 RAF and USAAF bombers prepared the way for D-Day by bombing key targets in Germany around the clock.

Even in England's darkest hours, dreams of invading and reconquering Europe were being born. The RAF Bomber Command began to carry the war to Germany. Soon RAF bombers were conducting nighttime raids on German cities. They were paying the Germans back for their cruel bombings of British cities.

Russia and the United States Join the Allies

In June 1941 Germany turned on its partner, Russia, and attacked. The mighty German armies drove deep into Russia until they were stopped by the Russian winter. Then in December 1941, following the Japanese attack on Pearl Harbor, Hawaii, the United States declared war on Japan and then on Germany and Italy. As a result the military strength of the Allies began to grow rapidly. U.S. Army and Army Air Force units began to arrive in Great Britain and supplies were sent to Russia to help fight the Germans.

A desert war between the British and the armies of

Germany and Italy (called the Axis powers) took place in North Africa. Germany carried on major campaigns on two fronts, against a determined Russian army in the north and against the British forces in Africa. And in 1942 the U.S. Army Air Force (USAAF) joined the RAF in bombing Germany. The Germans finally realized that the victory they planned on was not going to be an easy one.

Commando Raids — Practice for Invasion

In 1941, Great Britain did not have the resources to invade Europe. British army Special Service troops, called commandos, began sneak raids against the Germans. The first major raids took place against German forces in Norway. That nation had been invaded and conquered by Germany in April 1940. On March 4, 1941, a strong force of skilled commandos landed on the Lofoten Islands off the northwest coast of Norway. They destroyed valuable factories and supplies. They struck again on December 27, 1941, with equal success against Vaagson in southwest Norway.

On March 27 and 28, 1941, British Special Forces raided a large naval base at Saint-Nazaire, France, an important French port. They blew up dry docks and other harbor facilities. The mission was a great success. Germany had received another sample of the Allies' ability to strike back.

Russia Demands a Second Front in Europe

Meanwhile, Russia was suffering heavy losses. Joseph Stalin, the Russian leader, asked the Allies to attack German-occupied territory in Europe. This would take German troops away from the Russian front to fight elsewhere. But the Allies were not ready yet.

In April 1942 U.S. and British leaders met in London to discuss future plans. They agreed that an invasion of Europe by Allied forces from England would take place in the summer of 1943. However, the Russians continued calling for a "second front now."

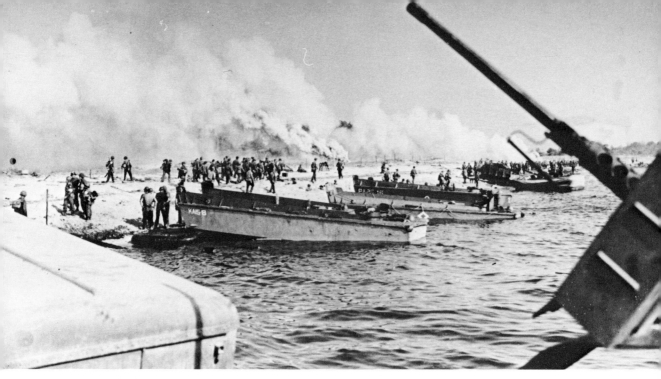

Allied commandos storm the beaches during the raid on Dieppe, France, in 1942.

The Dieppe Raid

Wanting to test German defenses and practice landings on the French coast, the Allies planned Operation Jubilee, against German troops at Dieppe, France. The raid was a disaster. Canadian, British and some American forces landed at Dieppe on August 19, 1942. They were to seize the city, a major communications center, drive off the defenders and capture enemy equipment and documents.

But the German defenders knew they were coming. A wild battle took place on the beaches, in the city and in the air above Dieppe. Completely outnumbered and disorganized, the Allied commandos had to withdraw after a day of bitter fighting. They had lost many men — more than 1,000 dead and 2,300 captured.

The Allies now knew that they were not prepared for a major assault on the beaches of France.

Landings in North Africa

Instead of landings in France, on November 8, 1942, British and American forces launched Operation Torch in North Africa. Although not the second front Stalin wanted, it was a giant and successful operation.

American, British and Free French forces, joining together, defeated the Axis forces in the African desert. The victory paved the way for an Allied invasion of Italy.

Meanwhile, plans were going ahead for the invasion of France. Beginning in 1942, Operation Bolero, the buildup of troops, equipment and supplies, was being carried out in Great Britain.

In January 1943 President Franklin Delano Roosevelt of the United States and Prime Minister Winston Churchill of Great Britain met in Casablanca in North Africa to make plans for future military action. It was finally decided that Italy would be the next target. The invasion of Europe from England would be postponed until 1944 when the Allies would be completely ready.

It was later decided that the invasion of France was to take place in the province of Normandy. It was given the code name Operation Overlord. The actual landings, called D-Day, were finally scheduled for the summer of 1944.

Thousands of American and British troops were landed in Africa during Operation Torch.

Chapter 2

THE INVASION ARMY

In February 1944 General Dwight D. Eisenhower was placed in charge of all Allied forces in Europe. His orders read: "You will enter the continent of Europe and, in conjunction with the other United Nations (all Allied nations), undertake operations aimed at the heart of Germany and the destruction of her armed forces." Operation Overlord and the scheduled invasion of Normandy were a result of this directive.

Great Britain had started making plans to return to the continent of Europe as early as 1940, when the Allies had been defeated in France. When the United States entered the war in December 1941, plans began to move ahead faster. The Allies immediately agreed that the conquest of Germany would come first, followed by the conquest of Japan. Germany was to be attacked from all sides — by Russia from the north and east and by combined RAF and USAAF bombing raids from the west. Allied armies in Italy would attack Germany from the south. Meanwhile, to support Overlord, the Atlantic Ocean had to be kept open so that convoys of Allied ships could deliver men and equipment to Great Britain.

Allied Planning

As General Eisenhower took command of Operation Overlord, he knew he had a terrible responsibility. If the invasion failed and Allied troops were driven off, the German position in France would become even stronger.

Western Europe might never be free from Nazi rule. Another invasion force would have to be built, or perhaps the Allied efforts would be shifted to the Far East to fight Japan instead. The war could drag on for years and either Great Britain or Russia could even ask for a separate peace.

The invasion of North Africa slowed the plans for Overlord. Allied commanders had to divide their efforts between building Allied strength in the British Isles and supporting the North African battles. Most supplies crossing the Atlantic were sent to Africa and very little were sent to England. Meanwhile, anticipating a cross-channel attack, Hitler ordered the German army to reinforce the French coastal defenses called the Atlantic Wall.

Invasion Plans Take Shape

In April 1943 British lieutenant general Frederick Morgan was made chief of staff of the Allied supreme commander, General Eisenhower. General Morgan's job was to prepare the actual invasion plans for Overlord. He had to coordinate all activities among the Americans, the British and the Russians. The Russians had to attack from the east as the British and American forces landed in France.

As Italy surrendered in 1943 and Germany began to weaken in that theater of war, the buildup of supplies in England began in earnest. Preparations for D-Day were finally well under way.

By the spring of 1944 General Eisenhower had an invasion force of some 600,000 troops. British, American, Canadian, Polish and Free French divisions were trained for the invasion. A force of more than 15,000 combat and transport aircraft and more than 5,000 ships was made ready for the invasion of France.

Tricking the Germans

One of the key elements of the total Overlord plan was to keep the Germans guessing where an invasion might

The Overlord invasion fleet was loaded weeks in advance at seaports all around the British Isles.

take place. A fake invasion force was gathered in England close to a narrow stretch of the English Channel, called Pas-de-Calais, near Calais, France. Large concentrations of troops and equipment were gathered there. They were actually the forces for a second invasion wave that would follow the landings at Normandy. The Germans thought the invasion would cross the channel near Calais.

Fake Plans and Cross-Channel Spies

Heavy movements of troops and other activities in the northern regions of the British Isles made the Germans think that Norway and Denmark might be invasion targets. At other times Allied activity made Hitler wonder if an invasion of the Balkan countries in southern Europe would be carried out from Italy and Africa. The German High Command was kept guessing. At no time were the Nazis prepared for the final invasion on the beaches of Normandy in June 1944.

At the same time special cross-channel exploratory raids were made to investigate the beaches of France. British Special Forces spied on German defenses on land and on the heavy beach and frogmen located underwater barriers that had been placed all along the French coast.

Enigma and Ultra

Enigma was the name of the German machine that created secret codes used for military communications. The Nazis thought no one could break these codes. However, early in the war the British were able to break Enigma-encoded messages. The information gained in this manner was called Ultra. The Germans never learned that their coded messages were being intercepted by the British. As a result, Ultra played a key role in helping the Allies know many German plans in advance.

During 1942 and 1943 the German U-boats (submarines)

USAAF P-47 Thunderbolt fighters at an airfield in Great Britain waiting for final assembly before being sent into combat against the Luftwaffe

A lone German soldier stands guard beneath one of Germany's big guns guarding the French coast.

were winning the Battle of the Atlantic. Allied convoys were being attacked constantly and hundreds of transports were sunk. Finally, mainly as a result of information acquired by means of Ultra, the wolf packs of German U-boats were being defeated.

From fall 1943 until D-Day, vast quantities of troops and supplies were delivered to England with only minor losses. More than 1,500,000 Allied troops and mountains of supplies had been landed in England to prepare for the coming invasion.

Germany Still Unprepared for Invasion

Hitler believed that the Allies had not decided where to land. As a result, German armed forces were spread over a wide area, not knowing where to concentrate their efforts. By May 15, General Eisenhower had made his final plans and D-Day was set for June 5, depending on the weather conditions that day.

Chapter 3

OPERATION NEPTUNE

Admiral Sir Bertram Ramsay of the Royal Navy was in command of all naval operations for D-Day and Overlord. He had developed a 1,200-page plan of operations. It controlled every activity for every ship for every hour of the days before, during and after D-Day. This was called Operation Neptune.

More than 5,000 ships from ports all around Great Britain put to sea during the week before D-Day. From tugboats to giant battleships, every ship had its job to do.

The 175,000-man D-Day invasion force and all of its equipment had to land at the right places and at the right times. Minesweepers had to clear the final landing route off Normandy of enemy explosive mines. The first wave of landing ships had to be funneled through an area just off the southern coast of England and about 100 miles north of France. This area was called Piccadilly Circus.

The Landing Craft

The invasion forces needed many craft, of different sizes and purposes, to land the invading army. The LCVP (Landing Craft Vehicles or Personnel) and the LCA (Landing Craft Assault) carried small groups of fighting men and small vehicles right onto the beaches. They were launched from large troop transports. LCIs (Landing Craft Infantry) carried over a hundred soldiers each right through the roaring surf to solid ground.

LSTs (Landing Ship Tank) were huge landing craft that

Protected from enemy dive-bombers by barrage balloons, a small part of the 5,000-ship D-Day invasion fleet crosses the English Channel.

carried heavy tanks and guns. As each LST sailed into the shallow waters of the beaches, the front of each ship would open up, ramps would drop and the troops and heavy equipment would roll out onto the beaches.

Hundreds of LCTs (Landing Craft Tank) and LCMs (Landing Craft Mechanized) were brought close to shore by large transports. Dropped into the sea from their mother ships, these craft brought tanks, guns and trucks to support the infantrymen who led the invasion.

Gooseberries and Mulberries

After Allied troops landed on the beaches of Normandy, reinforcements and supplies in huge quantities would have to follow. This could not be accomplished from the open sea. Docks and breakwaters would be needed. Immediately after D-Day landings, special barriers called gooseberries, made up of sunken ships and barges, were created just offshore from Normandy. Giant concrete-and-steel floating piers, called mulberries, were towed across the English Channel. They were sunk alongside the gooseberries to provide temporary docks to unload the supply ships from Great Britain.

Predawn Bombardment

A huge and powerful fleet of Allied warships was in position in the English Channel on June 5 to blast the Germans' defenses. More than 700 warships guarded the fleet of landing craft and support ships. Some 90 battleships, cruisers and destroyers from the Allied navies started their prelanding bombardment of the beaches in the early morning hours of June 6.

There were five landing beaches. Each location had to be bombed from the air and bombarded from the sea just before the first landing craft hit the beach. As the transports and landing craft approached Piccadilly Circus, the warships were ready to prepare the way.

On D-Day a U.S. Navy battleship fires a broadside of 16-inch shells aimed at German defenses on the French coast.

Men, tanks, guns and supplies pour ashore hour after hour and day after day on the beaches of Normandy.

At 3 A. M. German radar finally identified the approaching invasion fleet. All Nazi defenses in Normandy were alerted, and their giant guns opened fire. A number of minesweepers, destroyers and landing craft were sunk or damaged. Then the massive firepower of the entire Allied fleet rained a huge barrage of high explosives on the German defensive positions. The German batteries of guns, hit hard by the heavy bombardment, failed to stop the Allied landings.

As the landings took place on the five beaches of the Normandy coast, the giant support fleet was close behind. Wave after wave of courageous American, Canadian and British troops struggled ashore under heavy German fire. Casualties were heavy, but still more waves of landing craft stormed the beaches. The thousands of supply ships sailed close behind the landing forces. And the giant LSTs and LCMs brought more and more guns and tanks to help knock holes in the German defensive wall.

As D-Day ended, landing forces were firmly entrenched on all five beaches. Some 150,000 troops had been landed. The Nazi defenders were fighting back fiercely. If it had not been for the tremendous support of the combined Allied navies, the invasion could not have succeeded.

Chapter 4

D-DAY FROM THE AIR

The RAF and the USAAF also played key roles in the success of Overlord. Under the command of Air Chief Marshal Sir Trafford Leigh-Mallory, Allied planes bombed and strafed the enemy continually and landed airborne troops behind their lines.

Starting in the summer of 1943 and continuing into the early months of 1944, the Allied bomber commands had bombed German factories and Luftwaffe airfields. The German fighter forces had to be weakened both by destroying aircraft factories on the ground and defeating the Luftwaffe in the air.

Bombing raids were also made on key rail yards, railroads and highways. Allied heavy bombers and low-level fighter-bombers did everything they could to destroy bridges, airfields and lines of communication in France. They had to prevent reinforcements from reaching Normandy on D-Day. On the morning of D-Day Allied bombers dropped more than 1,700 tons of bombs on the Atlantic Wall that protected the Normandy beaches.

V-1 and V-2 Launch Sites Attacked

The Germans had been successful in developing two superweapons. Beginning in June 1944 the V-1 buzz bombs (flying bombs) regularly attacked London and other targets in England from well-hidden launch sites in France and Belgium. The Germans were also developing the V-2, a rocket that could carry huge loads of explosives with great

Dr. Wernher von Braun, the director of Germany's rocket program, suffered a broken arm during RAF raids against a V-2 assembly plant.

accuracy. If these weapons were launched against the highly compact D-Day landing forces it would be a disaster.

Under the command of Air Chief Marshal Sir Arthur "Bomber" Harris, a 50-plane raid successfully bombed V-2 factories in eastern Germany. That raid delayed the development of the V-2 until after D-Day. V-1 launch sites were also located and bombed heavily.

Eisenhower Given Control of Air Power

Until General Eisenhower was made supreme commander of the Allied forces for Overlord, the Allied air forces had their own plans for conducting the air war. However, General Eisenhower insisted on having complete control of all army, navy and air force activities if Overlord was to be successful.

The combined Allied air forces devoted their main efforts to attacking targets directly affecting the outcome of the landings in Normandy. During the final months before D-Day some 3,000 fighters and light bombers were used to attack enemy lines of communication. During the battle for Normandy they provided close air-ground support. High-flying heavy bombers continued their efforts to destroy key civilian and military targets within France and Germany.

Over 5,000 German aircraft had been destroyed during the year prior to D-Day, and more than 50 percent of Germany's war industry had been destroyed or damaged. The Allied superiority in the air over Normandy was so great that the Luftwaffe could do nothing to help stop the invasion. German troops, cut off from reinforcements and supplies, often lay helpless under Allied air attacks just before and during the critical battles leading up to the Allied breakout from the Normandy beachheads.

RAF Wellington medium bombers and U.S. P-51s (this one with RAF markings) played a major role in supporting the D-Day invasion.

Parachutes open overhead as waves of paratroopers land in France during the Normandy invasion.

Airborne Troops Prepare the Way

Shortly after midnight on June 6, U.S. and British airborne troops took off to land behind the German lines in Normandy. Three airborne divisions were involved in these early morning missions. A British force landed gliders and paratroopers behind the eastern end of the Normandy beaches. They destroyed bridges and knocked out key coastal German gun positions. Two U.S. airborne divisions landed at other points west of the beachheads with mixed success.

Bad flying weather and high winds caused many paratroopers to land way off target. However, most achieved their goals. They destroyed key German installations and prevented German troops from reaching the beaches.

From D-Day until the final breakout from Normandy, the Allied air forces dominated the skies over France and the English Channel. The Luftwaffe was never a threat. Without the close and constant support of the RAF and the USAAF, Operation Overlord would probably have failed.

Chapter 5

THE NORMANDY LANDINGS

After almost five long years of war the Allied forces based in England were ready to invade western Europe. Finally, in June 1944, under the command of General Eisenhower, a giant Allied army of 175,000 men would cross the English Channel. Their goal was to gain a foothold in France. They would then drive eastward toward Germany, destroying the Nazi army.

After years of preparation and the final months of planning, D-Day, the day of the invasion, was scheduled for June 5, 1944. But before daybreak on June 4, bad weather was forecast for the following 24 hours. All invasion activity was brought to a halt.

A Difficult Decision

General Eisenhower was faced with the most difficult decision of his career. The landings had to be made at low tide and in fairly good weather so that the troops could move safely from ships to shore. A full moon was necessary for the airborne landings early on D-Day morning. If the scheduled invasion was postponed even for a few days, the Allies would have to wait another month or more. And any delay would give the Germans more time to build up their defenses.

On the other hand, if General Eisenhower ordered the invasion to proceed and the weather remained bad, it could be a disaster. Casualties would be high. The German defenders could easily defeat a landing force already battered and torn by rough seas and hindered by cloudy and stormy skies. Allied aircraft would be kept on the ground, paratroop and glider missions would be canceled, and the invading troops would be without air support.

General Eisenhower studied the weather almost minute by minute during the daylight hours of June 4. Finally, he received a favorable weather forecast that evening at 9:30 P.M. The invasion would start at 6:30 A.M. on June 6, 1944.

Landing Forces Head for Normandy

As the weather began to clear on June 5, RAF and USAAF bombers increased their attacks on key targets in Normandy. British and American C-47 transport aircraft took off shortly after midnight. They carried American and British paratroopers and towed gliders full of British commandos and their equipment. These advance units were to destroy bridges, seize key enemy positions and

General Dwight D. Eisenhower shares his plans for victory with paratroopers in England just before they take off for France.

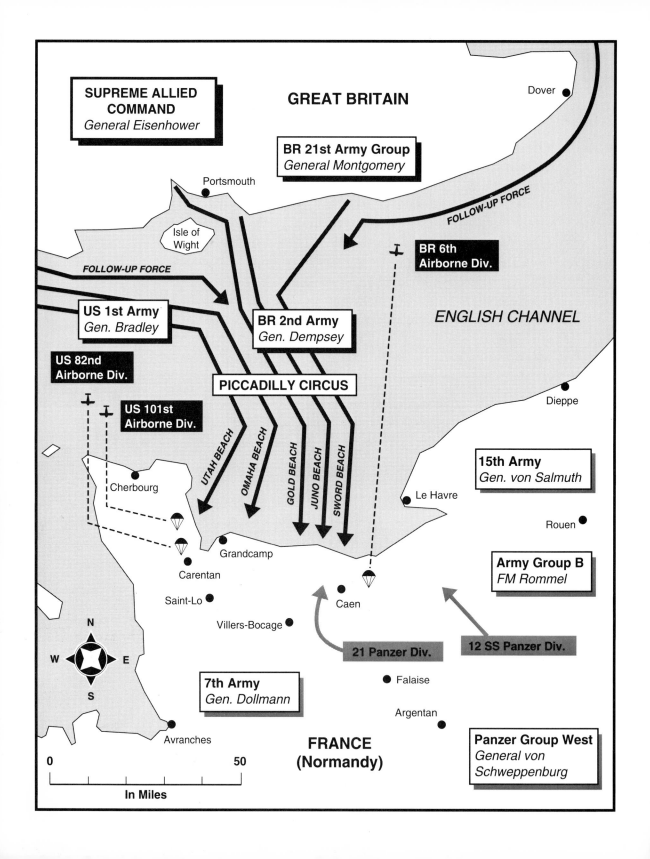

disrupt communications inland from the landing areas.

The supporting fleet of Allied warships drew close to shore and unleashed a gigantic barrage onto the beaches of Normandy. High-explosive shells and aerial bombs rained onto the German defenses.

At the same time, five separate landing forces left Piccadilly Circus. British general Sir Bernard Montgomery was in overall command of the landing forces. Two American groups of the U.S. 1st Army were commanded by General Omar Bradley. They were to land in Normandy on Utah Beach and Omaha Beach at the western end of the targeted area. The British 2nd Army, commanded by General Sir Miles Dempsey, headed toward the central and eastern Normandy beaches called Gold, Juno and Sword.

As the first landing craft approached the beaches, smoke flares were fired. These called for the warships to cease firing on the beach defenses. At 6:31 A.M. American troops were the first to land as they charged ashore on Utah Beach.

German Defenders Caught by Surprise

The German defense of France was under the command of Field Marshal Erwin Rommel. He had achieved fame as the Desert Fox in North Africa. But from Adolf Hitler on down, most German leaders were sure that the invasion would come near Calais. German forces that were in or near Normandy were stationed well inland. The destruction of German railroads, highways and bridges by Allied bombing delayed Nazi forces as they tried to respond to the invasion.

And the Luftwaffe was nowhere in sight. The Allies had complete control of the skies over Normandy. They bombed and machine-gunned the Atlantic Wall defenses continuously. The stray German fighters that tried to attack the Allied landing forces were quickly intercepted and destroyed by RAF Spitfire fighter aircraft.

However, as the hours of D-Day passed, German reinforcements moved toward the five beachheads. German defenders on the Atlantic Wall were finally fighting back fiercely.

Utah Beach

In the predawn hours of June 6, landing craft carrying some 1,200 American troops and equipment circled off Utah Beach. They were to lead and clear the way. Shells fired from Allied battleships roared overhead to explode on the beach defenses. B-26 Marauder bombers swooped in to drop more than 500 tons of bombs on the beach and German gun positions.

The first Utah Beach landing craft carried tanks and demolition experts. They were to clear away barricades, barbed wire, explosive mines and other obstacles. Much of this advance force landed safely. But some faced disaster. Some of the tanks were called DDs which stands for "dual drive." Held afloat by special flotation gear, they had propellers that would push the heavy monsters as they floated toward shore. When their caterpillar treads touched bottom the regular power system would take over. But the flotation system on some tanks failed and they sank like rocks.

Other landing craft were hit by enemy fire or were damaged by underwater mines. But most reached shore safely. Landing on a stretch of beach only one mile long, the troops met little enemy resistance. By day's end they had expanded their beachhead to four miles across and five miles inland. Some 23,000 men had landed on Utah Beach with fewer than 200 casualties.

The flail tank, used to explode buried explosive mines, was just one of the "funny" tanks developed for special jobs.

A landing craft loaded with American troops surges toward the beaches of Normandy.

Omaha Beach Heavily Defended

As troops stormed ashore at Utah Beach, another American force was landing just 15 miles to the east. Landings there were to be as difficult as Utah Beach was easy. Guarded by high bluffs, Omaha Beach was a giant trap.

Wave after wave of landing craft came ashore on 2,000 yards of beach in heavy surf. Hitting the beach on the run, the invading troops were soon pinned down by heavy enemy fire. Again the DD tanks were in trouble. Launched too far from shore, several dozen sank. Without the heavy firepower of these tanks, the troops dug in on the beach were at the mercy of vicious crossfire from well-hidden German artillery and machine-gun positions.

Trapped on the narrow beach by 125-foot-high rock cliffs, the first waves of Americans were being cut to pieces. There were only a few places that offered natural access to the level ground above. U.S. Rangers set out to climb the cliffs at these points to silence the German guns. Following a fierce battle with Nazi defenders, the Rangers were successful and secured the west end of Omaha Beach.

Temporary cloud cover had cut down on bomber and fighter support. Many more landing craft were swamped in the icy waters of the English Channel. Troops on the beach were under heavy fire for most of the day. Finally, due to heroic individual and group action, the embattled U.S. forces climbed the cliffs and slowly moved inland.

Omaha Beach was defended by crack German troops that had survived the predawn naval and aerial bombardments. The landing areas were filled with American dead and wounded. The only outside help for the battered Americans was from the naval guns firing from warships standing just offshore.

Finally, as darkness fell on D-Day, the Americans began advancing by inches all along the German line. One German defensive position after another was knocked out. By night-

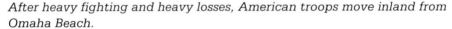

After heavy fighting and heavy losses, American troops move inland from Omaha Beach.

fall the Americans controlled only about six miles of Omaha Beach and had advanced two miles inland at the farthest point. It was far less than planned. But they were on the beach to stay. They spent a cold, wet and sleepless night in their foxholes and made ready to fight another day. Some 55,000 men had been landed on Omaha Beach but at a terrible price. More than 4,500 American troops had been killed or wounded.

British and Canadians Land to the East

Like the Americans, the British and Canadians landed with mixed results. Their three target areas covered beaches about 20 miles long. The British landing on Gold Beach was led by well-trained armored units that moved the forces on and off the beaches quickly. Meeting resistance as they advanced inland, the troops fought a steady battle with defending Germans.

Juno Beach, just a few miles to the east, offered a lot more trouble. Underwater obstacles and mines — along with rough water — slowed the landings. After reaching the beaches, Canadian commandos headed inland. Accompanied by Free French troops to help with the local residents, the Canadians charged toward their main target, the city of Caen, 20 miles inland. Although stopped in this effort, they joined up with the Gold Beach forces before the day was over.

Sword Beach in Trouble

The British invasion forces landing on Sword Beach were the only ones bothered by German naval activity. An alert German navy commander had ordered E-boats into action. These high-speed motor-torpedo boats darted toward the landing craft and launched torpedoes as they approached. Fortunately, they sank only one ship, with minor damage to others as the landing craft sped toward the beach.

The landings proceeded so rapidly that major traffic

jams occurred as the beaches became congested. As a result, the second and third waves of troops could not advance. British troops moving inland met heavy resistance. However, as major enemy obstacles were overcome, the troops began to move off the beach. Special commando groups joined up with airborne troops that had landed earlier. By the end of the second day troops from Sword had joined up with those from Juno and Gold. They presented a solid line of defense.

The British made excellent use of their armored strength, particularly a group of tanks called funnies. These included the DD amphibious tanks and "flail" tanks that used rotating attachments with long heavy chains. Mounted on the front of tanks, these "flails" struck the ground before advancing tanks and troops and exploded land mines. The British also used flat-topped tanks called alligators, which carried small bridge sections. This type of tank could position itself in a deep ditch or similar obstacle. It would then unfold its bridge sections to permit other tanks and vehicles to cross over.

German Command Confused

The German High Command was unprepared and confused by lack of orders from Hitler. An entire panzer division of crack German troops was awaiting orders to counterattack. Even after it was certain that an invasion was

Heavy Allied bombing attacks had ruined French roads, almost paralyzing enemy troop movements, as the Nazis tried to fight off the Allied invasion.

A wounded U.S. soldier is helped aboard a landing craft that will take him to a ship bound for England and safety.

underway, no orders came. When German troops near the beachheads finally went into action in midmorning, they were faced with hard-fighting Allied forces.

Field Marshal Rommel was on vacation several hundred miles away in Germany. He wasn't informed of the invasion of Normandy until hours after it had begun. The German High Command still believed the landing would come elsewhere. They refused to order reserves into action and kept badly needed divisions as far away as Paris. Hitler was not informed of the invasions until almost noon on D-Day. At no time that day did German defenders on the Atlantic Wall win a major battle against the invading Allies.

Invasion a Limited Success

The Allies had succeeded in landing at five different locations. They had reached many of their objectives and were advancing inland from all five beaches. But as darkness fell on D-Day, German counterattacks were taking their toll. The major targets had not been reached. Some 2,500 brave Allied soldiers and sailors had died and thousands more were wounded. But some 150,000 troops had been landed successfully, and huge quantities of supplies and equipment were piling up on the beaches. Operation Overlord was underway.

Chapter 6

FIGHTING IN NORMANDY

Following the successful D-Day landings, the Allies spent the remainder of June 1944 landing reinforcements and supplies and driving slowly inland. The Allies were fighting to expand their beachheads and the Germans were fighting to stop them. While the American, Canadian and British forces were being strengthened by the hour, the Nazi army was operating under severe handicaps.

First of all, Hitler believed that the Normandy landings were not the real invasion. As a result, he would not permit panzer divisions held in reserve to enter the battle. When he did, late in the afternoon on D-Day, the bomb-damaged transportation system in France seriously delayed the movement of troops and equipment toward the beachheads.

Linking the Beachheads

As the sun rose on June 7 the Allies were securely dug in on all five beachheads. Both the British and Americans had joined up with their airborne units that had landed behind German lines early D-Day morning. The immediate problem was to extend and strengthen the beach positions so that more troops and supplies could be landed.

On Utah and Omaha beaches the Americans, although successful in their initial efforts, were disorganized and running behind schedule. Less than half the equipment and supplies had been landed. Tanks, heavy artillery and a wide range of other weapons were badly needed.

A pilot's-eye view of Allied gliders that have landed amid the hedge-rows of Normandy

Scrapping the initial plan to occupy the entire Cotentin Peninsula, General Bradley ordered the Utah and Omaha beaches to be merged. This would provide a stronger defense and prevent the German panzers from driving a wedge between the beachheads. On June 12, the city of Carenton at the base of the Cotentin Peninsula was captured. That same day Utah and Omaha forces joined together.

During this period American forces from Omaha Beach and British forces from Gold Beach moved inland rapidly and captured the town of Bayeux, closing another gap in the 20-mile-long beachhead. By June 13 all five beachheads were firmly joined. The Allies now presented a solid front against German defenders from Carentan on the west to the German-held town of Caen on the east.

Battles of the Bocage — Hedgerows

Normandy was French farm country. Almost all of the battle for Normandy was fought across thousands of family farms that were just a few acres in size. And each field was separated from the next by the *bocage* — sunken lanes and hedgerows of tightly knit bushes, trees and tangled vines. Unable to see through the hedgerows, American and British infantry and tanks were met with fire from hidden German tanks and machine-gun nests.

The first tragic victims of the *bocage* were American and British gliders. Hedgerows so close together made landing a glider safely almost impossible. Casualties were high as one glider after another splintered and broke apart hitting the hedgerows. As slowly moving Allied tanks tried to climb over the *bocage*, the tank crews could not see their attackers and were easy prey for Nazi antitank gunners.

Hedgerow Cutters Save the Day

Not recognizing the problems presented by hedgerows, the Americans and the British were completely unprepared

Sharp-toothed hedgecutters were welded to the front of Allied tanks so that they could cut their way through Normandy hedgerows.

to overcome these natural barriers. Heavy losses mounted. Finally, a young American tank crewman saved the day. He welded a heavy iron fork made of sharp steel blades to the front of a tank. Moving forward at a good rate of speed, the tank easily sliced through the hedgerows. Tanks could now meet the German defenders head-on with guns blazing. Soon, most Allied tanks fighting in Normandy were equipped with hedgerow cutters.

After linking up with Omaha Beach forces, the 82nd and 101st airborne divisions struck west from Utah Beach. By June 18 the Americans had cut all the way across the Cotentin Peninsula, trapping the German forces stationed on that narrow point of land.

Fighting along the Normandy front was slowed by a violent storm on the English Channel in mid-June. However, by June 22, after the storm was over, the Allies had more than 20 divisions in position in Normandy, against 16 German divisions. The Americans were rapidly approaching the vital seaport of Cherbourg at the tip of the Cotentin Peninsula and the city of Saint-Lo about 20 miles inland from Omaha Beach. To the east, the British were fighting a determined but losing battle to capture the main transportation center and airfield at the heavily defended city of Caen.

The Battles for Cherbourg and Caen

Field Marshal Rommel recognized that it would be impossible to hold the Cotentin Peninsula and the seaport of Cherbourg. He asked permission to withdraw and fight the Allies in more favorable territory. Hitler refused.

Using their vastly superior armored forces and air power, the Allies defeated three German divisions and captured that valuable peninsula and Cherbourg, but not before the defending German commander had ordered the destruction of all dock and harbor facilities in that seaport city. However, within a few weeks Allied reinforcements and supplies were pouring ashore at Cherbourg over roadways built on top of sunken German ships and burned-out docks.

To the east the British launched Operation Epsom on June 26. It was an all-out attempt to drive the Germans from Caen. The seesaw battle lasted for five days until fresh German SS panzer divisions arrived and forced the British to withdraw.

At this point the German commanders, Field Marshal Rommel and Field Marshal Gerd von Rundstedt, met with Hitler to plan future strategy. The German dictator still did not understand that his armies were losing in Normandy. Rommel and von Rundstedt recommended that they withdraw from Normandy and set up a strong defense line

A German gun position in Cherbourg lies in ruins after receiving a direct hit during Allied bombardment.

U.S. infantry troops take cover as they attack Nazi positions somewhere in Normandy.

farther inland. Hitler turned down that idea and ordered them to attack and drive the Allies back into the sea. Von Rundstedt was removed from command and his replacement, Field Marshal Gunther von Kluge, and Rommel continued the losing battle for Normandy.

As June drew to a close, the Allies had been in Normandy for 24 days. They had captured Cherbourg and all of the Cotentin Peninsula, but had driven no more than 20 miles inland at any point along the D-Day beachheads. Drastic action was needed.

Operations Cobra and Goodwood

As the month of July began, General Bradley's 1st U.S. Army was trying to drive southward near the key city of Saint-Lo. However, the Germans had built up their forces in that area and were fighting fiercely. Meeting stiff resistance, the U.S. 1st Army was at a standstill and was suffering heavy casualties.

General Bradley began making plans and started massing his troops for a new major effort. The planned breakout from Normandy was given the code name Cobra and was scheduled for the end of July.

To take pressure off the 1st Army as it prepared for Cobra, the British increased their activity to the east. They launched another major attack to capture the city of Caen on July 9. This was called Operation Goodwood. It would be a combined effort to secure Caen and to attack eastward in an attempt to break out of Normandy.

Operation Goodwood — Success and Failure

On July 18 Allied bombers dropped more than 7,000 tons of bombs near Caen and on the German defenses at the eastern end of the expanding beachhead. British armor, achieving early success, drove past Caen and continued to drive eastward. But the Germans rushed in reinforcements from all up and down the Normandy line, bringing the British advance to a halt. On that same day, taking advantage of the resulting weakening of German defenses to the west, American troops captured Saint-Lo.

Goodwood had succeeded in drawing German defenders away from Saint-Lo but at the same time had failed to accomplish a breakout from Normandy. Now Operation Cobra was ready to proceed.

Hitler Bomb Plot — Rommel Wounded

The German army was in serious trouble throughout France. Not only were they losing in Normandy, but also the French and German transportation systems was in a shambles. As many as 1,800 trains trying to bring reinforcements and supplies to Normandy were blocked by bomb-damaged railroads and bridges. At the same time, Field Marshal Rommel was seriously wounded when his staff car was strafed by RAF aircraft.

But most disconcerting to the Nazis was an attempt to kill their leader, Adolf Hitler. On July 20, a plot planned and

A U.S. antitank crew in action against retreating German troops as the breakout from Normandy begins.

hatched by a group of German generals failed. Hitler was injured by a bomb in the assassination attempt but survived. Most of those who had conspired to carry out the assassination were caught and executed. They had hoped to take over the German government and end the war. The Nazi High Command and Hitler, though badly shaken, were still in charge.

Operation Cobra Gets Underway

The time had come to achieve the planned breakout of Normandy. General Bradley was completely responsible for the planning and execution of Cobra. It was to take place when and where the Germans were weakest. It also was to break through at a point that would offer good highways and open fields for a rapid advance. The plan also called for the maximum use of Allied air support. On July 25 Operation Cobra was launched exactly as planned.

The Allied air force used 2,500 aircraft to carpet-bomb an area about three miles square just west of Saint-Lo. The Allied aircraft strafed enemy troops and dropped more than 5,000 tons of bombs in that small area. German resistance there was almost completely wiped out. The German defenders were in full retreat following the heavy bombings. Because of bad weather and a misunderstanding between Allied commanders, a number of U.S. troops had been bombed by mistake.

But Cobra was underway. American armor advanced at full speed through the hole in the enemy lines. On July 26 and 27, U.S. troops had advanced past the Saint-Lo line and were deep behind German lines. They drove south and east into France. The German forces in western Normandy were thoroughly beaten and about to collapse. The breakout from Normandy had begun.

A USAAF B-26 Marauder delivers a bombload on German positions during the Normandy invasion.

Chapter 7

BREAKOUT FROM NORMANDY

As the Normandy breakout began, the U.S. 1st Army advanced rapidly to the south and west. At that time the Allied forces in Normandy were reorganized. A new 12th Army Group was formed under General Bradley to control the U.S. armies leading the Normandy breakout into the Brittany peninsula. General Montgomery still commanded the 21st Army Group made up of British and Canadian forces that were to drive south and east from the original beachheads.

A new U.S. 3rd Army had been forming in deep secrecy and waiting to enlarge upon the Normandy breakout. It was commanded by "Old Blood and Guts" General George Patton. General Patton's forces advanced with lightning speed into Brittany to the south and west. The 1st Army continued fighting in Normandy.

German Counterattack in Normandy

Field Marshal von Kluge now commanded the Nazi armies in Normandy. Hitler ordered von Kluge to attack to the west. His goal was to cut off General Patton's army and then attack northward against the U.S. 1st Army in Normandy. The Germans attacked on August 6 with four panzer divisions. But the U.S. forces had been warned by Ultra and were ready for the attack. Fighting against vastly superior U.S. ground forces, the German attackers were also strafed and bombed from the air. Within a week this German attack had failed.

While the German counterattack was underway, General Patton's forces were thrusting deep into Brittany. By August 7 they had advanced over 100 miles to the French Atlantic coast. The U.S. 3rd Army now controlled the entire Brittany peninsula except for the seaport of Brest, which held out against the Allies for six weeks. The U.S. forces were ready to direct their attacks to the east toward northern France and Germany.

The Falaise Pocket

Heavy fighting continued in Normandy. Although General von Kluge's counterattack had been defeated, he still had a large German army and several panzer divisions in southeastern Normandy. Retreating after the failed westward attack, the German army soon found itself surrounded on three sides. There were U.S. forces on the west, British and Canadian forces on the north, and General Patton's U.S. 3rd Army on the south. A huge German army was about to be trapped.

A German tank crew surrenders to U.S. infantrymen.

A Free Polish armored force serving with the British in Normandy helps close the gap at Falaise.

Although the Germans were almost surrounded, there was still a gap about 20 miles wide between the French towns of Falaise and Argentan. If the Germans withdrew rapidly, they could escape the trap and get out of the Falaise pocket. The Canadians advancing from the north were stopped by hard-fighting panzer divisions. Patton's forces did not press home an attack from the south because of shortages of supplies.

Finally the Canadians captured Falaise, and the German forces of almost 100,000 men were trying to stream out of the trap as fast as they could. Only some 30,000 Germans escaped. More than 50,000 were taken prisoner and 10,000 or more were killed. It was a stunning defeat for the Germans, which ended all resistance in Normandy.

Allies Land in Southern France

Part of General Eisenhower's grand plan for the conquest of France and Germany called for an invasion of the south of France. On August 15 Operation Dragoon began with the landing of U.S. and Free French forces on the Mediterranean coast of southern France. The German forces, badly weakened by withdrawal of troops and equipment to Normandy, were unprepared. An immediate success, this Allied invasion force drove quickly northward, with the German defenders in full retreat.

French and U.S. Troops Enter Paris

General Eisenhower had decided to bypass Paris, the capital of France, to avoid a bitter battle that might destroy that beautiful city. He knew that this decision would leave the citizens of Paris still under German rule, but at the same time it would spare them the destruction of a street-by-street battle. However, the French people took matters into their own hands. Quickly building barricades, they prepared to battle the German occupation forces.

On August 19 men and women of the French Resistance, the FFI (French Forces of the Interior), rose up and started fighting the German forces that occupied Paris. The German commander immediately called for an armistice. However, due to a breakdown in communications, the French Resistance fighters continued to attack the Germans. The Germans were forced to fight back.

Hitler, maddened even further by continuing defeats, ordered the German commander in Paris to destroy the city. But the commander loved Paris and agreed to a temporary truce. At the same time French and U.S. forces were rushing at high speed toward Paris to aid the FFI.

Free French and U.S. forces entered the liberated city on August 25. Later that evening, General Charles de Gaulle, the leader of the Free French government, arrived to return Paris to French control.

American troops march down the Champs Elysees in Paris in a victory parade following the liberation of the French capital.

Normandy Breakout Complete

As August 1944 drew to a close, the Allied armies had successfully completed Operation Overlord. Within a few more days all German forces would be driven from France. The victorious U.S. armies were in control of south and central France. British and Canadian forces, moving east from Normandy, were occupying all of northern France. The German armies had retreated in a complete rout and were regrouping their forces in Germany.

On September 1, General Eisenhower moved the headquarters of the Allied forces to mainland Europe. The Allies were preparing their next thrust toward the heart of Germany. They would continue to fight against a battered and confused — but still strong — Nazi army, controlled by its fanatic leader, Adolf Hitler.

GLOSSARY

Allies The nations that joined together during World War II to defeat Germany, Italy and Japan: Great Britain, United States, the Soviet Union (Russia) and France.

armistice A mutually-consented temporary stop in fighting between hostile armies.

artillery Large weapons such as cannon, howitzers and missile launchers suitably mounted and fired by a crew.

Axis The partnership of Germany, Italy and Japan during World War II.

commando A small fighting force specially trained to make quick, destructive attacks against enemy positions.

E-boat Small, high-speed German torpedo and patrol boats.

frogman A swimmer equipped with underwater breathing and other equipment to conduct demolition of enemy targets during wartime.

glider An engineless aircraft that is towed by a powered aircraft. Upon reaching its destination, the glider is cut loose and glides to a landing.

Nazi A person or idea of the German National Socialist party.

panzer A German tank.

paratrooper An infantryman trained and equipped to parachute from an airplane.

radar Radio equipment that detects airplanes and ships and determines their distance, speed and altitude. Short for RAdio Detection And Ranging.

torpedo A self-propelled underwater missile that explodes on contact with a target.

U-boat A German submarine, short for *Unterseeboot*, or undersea boat.

INDEX